I08O5057

IMAGES
of America

KNOXVILLE *in* WORLD WAR II

Ed Hooper

ARCADIA
PUBLISHING

Copyright © 2006 by Ed Hooper
ISBN978-0-7385-4320-8

Published by Arcadia Publishing
Charleston, South Carolina

Printed in the United States of America

Library of Congress Catalog Card Number: 2006926352

For all general information contact Arcadia Publishing at:
Telephone 843-853-2070
Fax 843-853-0044
E-mail sales@arcadiapublishing.com
For customer service and orders:
Toll-Free 1-888-313-2665

Visit us on the Internet at www.arcadiapublishing.com

This book is dedicated to the brave men and women of Knoxville who served their nation in World War II at home, on the job, and on the battlefields of Africa, Asia, the Middle East, and Europe.

IMAGES
of America

KNOXVILLE *in* WORLD WAR II

ON THE COVER: The Appalachian Mills in Knoxville was one of many businesses in the city that saw working hours and production leap as the nation entered World War II. The sudden demands for electrical power from industry in wartime led to the continued growth of the Tennessee Valley Authority's hydroelectric dam building projects in East Tennessee. (Photograph courtesy of Tennessee Valley Authority.)

CONTENTS

Acknowledgments

I would like to acknowledge the following people and organizations for their assistance in acquiring these photographs: F. A. Blankenship, the Tennessee Valley Authority, the Library of Congress, the Salvation Army Southern Historical Center, Avon Rollins of the Beck Cultural Exchange Center, the Knoxville American Red Cross, Fred Reagan, Bill Henderson, Kathy Jones, Sen. Tim Burchett, Sen. Jamie Woodson, and the Tennessee National Guard.

Above all, I would like to express my sincere gratitude to World War II veteran Charles Burchett of Knoxville, without whom this would not have been possible.

INTRODUCTION

On September 16, 1940, a secret file known as the "Tennessee Plan" was activated from the Tennessee National Guard Adjutant General's office under orders of then-governor Prentice Cooper. For more than a year, the Ivy League–educated governor had been putting the state's house in order and preparing for the inevitable. The winds of world war blowing from Asia and Europe had fueled the flames of anxiety in North America for more than five years, and Governor Cooper wanted to make sure Tennessee was prepared for what was to come. A massive armory building program had been enacted, the Tennessee Adjutant General (TAG) office had reworked the National Guard, and the groundwork was laid for the greatest call-up of citizen soldiers in American history.

On December 7, 1941, the city of Knoxville was in the early evening hours when the first radio reports broke about the Japanese bombing of Pearl Harbor. Among the 2,395 known dead were Knoxvillians and East Tennesseans serving in the armed forces in Hawaii. There was more anger than disbelief, as local sons would be among the dead of Pearl Harbor. But it would become much more than a day of mourning for the city of Knoxville. It would be an event that would reshape the face of the city and the entire East Tennessee region. While the area was still largely an agricultural one, the wheels of industry quickly gained new traction, and people accustomed to the farms and fields found new opportunities in the factories and businesses that sprang to life in the Tennessee Valley.

When asked today, many people think Knoxville was unique because of its proximity to Oak Ridge and the Manhattan Project. The establishment of the Oak Ridge Nuclear Laboratory, however, and the secret weapons development would not be a part of Knoxville lore for more than a year after the attack on Pearl Harbor, and by then, the city would be well on its way to making its own mark on World War II history.

World War I had put the small Appalachian city on the map. Its efforts with the American Red Cross, businesses like the Fulton Sylphon Company, and the soldiers, sailors, pilots, and civilians who had volunteered so freely earned Knoxville a place in the annals of American military history. With the city powered up by the Tennessee Valley Authority, those same resources 20 years later would be called upon again, and this time, the effort would be truly monumental and life would never be the same afterward.

Through the hydroelectric dam projects of the Tennessee Valley Authority (TVA) and the growing demand for power, Knoxville had already seen a massive influx of people—many referred to in the city halls as "mountain whites," who had been forced from homes they held for generations in the Smoky Mountains and moved to Knoxville, where they tried to make a living for their families.

Once again, the Fulton Sylphon Company, joined by others like the Aluminum Company of America (ALCOA), the Dempster Machine Shop, Camel Tent Company, and the numerous textile mills, would keep the railroad yards humming with activity. Traditional employees were scarce, and women would become a vibrant and necessary part of the Knoxville workforce—making contributions to the war effort one will never find in the history texts of the era.

Government and military agencies would also locate numerous training camps, bases, and facilities in the region. While no soldier trained on Tennessee soil in World War I, more than two million would be trained on the rivers, in the mountains, and in the valleys of Tennessee in World War II. There were beach landings made at Memphis, river operations on the Cumberland, and paratrooper operations in the mountainous east. Because of this, the electrical power resources of TVA, and the hundreds of thousands of Tennesseans serving in both military and civilian capacity, the state became known as the "inner citadel" of the United States, and at the heart of that citadel was Knoxville.

By and large, however, it was the sheer number of male citizens called up for active duty that rocked Knoxville to its core. No family was left untouched, and everyone had brothers, husbands, and sons in the armed forces. As in wars past, Knoxville was a leader in maintaining Tennessee's volunteer tradition, and Knoxvillians served in every theater of operation. It is still a point of pride for many today who claim the sun never set on a Tennessee soldier in World War II.

With all this activity from local, state, and federal governments, businesses, and other forces, one would think finding photographs of Knoxville in this era would be an easy task. It was not. Most families did not own cameras, rationing limited their ability to purchase film, and the photographs that were taken have faded, been lost through the generations, or were simply tossed aside. This collection of photographs was gathered over a period of time from family members, businesses, and organizations and lent in the spirit of remembrance and dedication that the efforts of all who participated never be forgotten. It was the era of hometowns, and most men were remembered by where they came from in the United States and not their names. In a lot of these photographs are unnamed Knoxvillians, and hopefully through the publication of this book, we can finally put names on the faces peering from the past.

These men and women were veterans of one of the last times in world history where uniformed armies stood face-to-face and fought to the death to establish justice and preserve a way of life free from the dictators and tyranny of the time. This is Knoxville's story in World War II through the eyes of the organizations and businesses that were in the city and from the men who fought overseas.

One

Knoxville Goes to War

Knoxville awakened December 8, 1941, to the news of the Pearl Harbor attack and waited to hear what the United States' response was going to be. Almost immediately, men began lining up at recruiting offices downtown to enlist, and companies began bracing for shortages and preparing to go into wartime production.

Knoxville had felt the effects of the Great Depression of the 1930s, but new industries had also found roots in the city and were starting to grow. The Tennessee River was being brought under control through the dam-building projects, and the quality of life in a largely rural East Tennessee had actually improved because of it.

Small businesses were also able to survive and thrive in the city. Government contracts and jobs aided their growth. The Tennessee Valley Authority had established its headquarters in Knoxville, and newer industries requiring a steady, uninterrupted power supply to operate them now had it at their disposal. Agriculture still ruled supreme in Knox County as it did elsewhere in Tennessee.

As World War II gripped Knoxville, the labor market started shrinking immensely. The young men who hadn't volunteered were being called up for service. The workforce numbers nose-dived, and employers found themselves hard-pressed for labor.

The city was traditionally a major textile center and one of the South's premier growing industrial bases. Knoxville companies were already working on more than $2 million in prewar military projects when the war began, and with demands increasing, they joined a list of industries requiring expansion rather than a depletion of personnel.

To compensate, women moved into factory and administrative work—assuming roles in the workforce reserved in the past exclusively for men. "Rosie the Riveter" was a nationwide image for most Americans. In Knoxville, "Suzie the Sewer" was her counterpart, and it was far more than uniforms. There were tents, canteen covers, ammo belts, backpacks, and every other piece of fabric that fit on a soldier, sailor, ship, or paratrooper. They spun it into fabric at the mills and then shipped it to assemblers at other companies across town.

Men who were too old for military service or unable to serve volunteered for the Tennessee State Guard, reentered the workforce, or served in governmental jobs created by the demands of war.

The infrastructure that supported the American war machine in Knoxville would be retooled many times in succeeding years to keep pace with the differing demands.

The Appalachian Mills in Knoxville was a major producer of textiles in the city. The factory was one of the largest in the South. Wartime production pushed this factory as well as others in the city to operate day and night.

The mills were a big part of the region's economy for generations. Although the equipment was outdated at many of the factories, World War II rationing and the heavy emphasis on military industries pushed owners to improvise and keep the mills in operation. This often meant cannibalizing old machinery to repair the newer ones, and many factories were strained to meet their production goals.

Knoxville's downtown business section changed little during the war. This photograph was taken in 1943 looking at Regas Restaurant on Gay Street. The restaurant was one of most popular eating places in the city. (Photograph courtesy of Bill Regas.)

The Dempster Brothers Company on Springdale Avenue was one of the key military industries in the city. Prior to World War II, the company produced waste disposal systems that were seen in every American shipyard, harbor, and military base around the world. Their most famous patent was for the Dempster Dumpster. The three brothers who ran the plant were, from left to right, John Dempster, Tom Dempster, and George Dempster. (Photograph courtesy of Tom Dempster.)

During the war, Dempster Brothers turned to making pontoons that were used on seaplanes and portable docks. They were designed to fit tightly together and compartmentalized to take abuse, so if one was struck by enemy fire, the others would support the dock. By war's end, the company had produced more than 400,000 pontoons. (Photograph courtesy of Tom Dempster.)

Mass transit was not available to many people who worked in Knoxville, and people were encouraged to never operate an automobile without passengers to conserve fuel. The Dempster Brothers, like other companies, would transport their employees to and from work. (Photograph courtesy of Tom Dempster.)

Zinc mining was important to the war engines of the United States. The zinc mines in Mascot churned out the ore that was used for industry and, during World War II, to make pennies since copper was needed for manufacturing.

While hydroelectricity was powering up the Tennessee Valley, it was only part of the equation for generating electricity. Coal was necessary for the other power plants, and it poured out of East Tennessee. During World War II, mining was one of the jobs considered so important that miners were often exempted from military service.

Westin Fulton was the founder of the Fulton Sylphon Company (see Images of America: *Knoxville* [Arcadia, 2003] chapter "The Can Do Company"). During World War II, the company made countless components for bombing sites and military weaponry. The avid toy maker is regarded as one of Tennessee's greatest inventors, and his development of the seamless bellows spun off so many inventions the U.S. Patent Office had to give it a special section.

The Fulton Sylphon Company's work in World War II would earn the company the Army-Navy "E" Award with five stars. It was the highest award for excellence given to any manufacturer.

Agriculture was traditionally the main economic machine of Knox County. This photograph of House Mountain, which is the highest point in the county, shows farming methods had changed little over the generations in the region.

This photograph shows a Knox County farmer on his tractor in 1942. The industrialization of agriculture increased the productivity of family farms and reduced the number of workers a farmer needed to tend labor-intensive crops.

This is a photograph of the Broadacres Dairy Farm off of Clinton Highway in Knox County taken in 1942. The introduction of electric milking machines was a modern miracle to dairy farmers in the region. It allowed them to milk more cows in less time and reduced the manpower needed for a dairy operation.

Putting family farms on the electrical grid in Tennessee was sometimes a tough sell for TVA. This photograph of Lena Weigel was taken to illustrate new electrical appliances available to people in Knox County thanks to the steady power supply provided by the government agency.

This photograph was taken in the 1940s to illustrate how the power supplied by TVA to Knoxville helped companies succeed and increased the quality of living by offering better-paying jobs for skilled laborers.

This is a refrigerated river barge in 1942. It was designed and built by the TVA and the University of Tennessee to encourage the fruit and vegetable freezing industry and the marketing of agricultural products over the developing inland waterways system. (Photograph courtesy of the Library of Congress.)

Constructing the dam required massive equipment and men working high off the ground. With all the possibilities for mishaps, TVA maintained a commendable safety record. (Photograph courtesy of Tennessee Valley Authority.)

When completed, Fort Loudon Dam provided another burst of energy to the power grid. In addition, Fort Loudon Lake, which was formed by the dam, would become a destination point for many Knoxville residents. Boating and other water recreation activities would provide another boost to the local economy. (Photograph courtesy of Tennessee Valley Authority.)

This is a part of the 1,300-man 7 a.m.-to-3 p.m. shift that worked to construct Fort Loudon Dam. Because of the urgent need for power to fuel industry in East Tennessee during World War II, two shifts worked night and day to build the dam.

This photograph depicts the dam-building process at Coffer Dam of Fort Loudon. Massive amounts of dirt, steel, and wood were needed to build forms that would hold the concrete that made up the walls of the dam.

Construction equipment was big business in Knoxville because of the ongoing building projects in the region. It was one industry that rushed to keep up with demand, and during World War II, heavy equipment mechanics were vital as rationing meant little new equipment was manufactured.

This photograph shows TVA trucks transporting prefabricated housing to the construction site at Fontana Dam. In the background is the Louisville and Nashville (L&N) Train Station in downtown Knoxville. The prefabricated houses were delivered by rail to Knoxville and transported to the site in Western North Carolina. (Photograph courtesy of Tennessee Valley Authority.)

Employee morale and keeping on schedule were major goals of TVA. The wartime poster was a common site at dam construction sites throughout the region. The reference to aluminum was to illustrate the importance of Fontana Dam to the Aluminum Company of America (ALCOA), which was located in nearby Maryville, Tennessee.

In World War II, traffic on the Tennessee River was constant, and it was not unusual to see dozens of barges like this one transporting a variety of products and freight. For Knoxvillians, it was a new sight, as the river had always been one of fluctuating levels and unable to support year-round traffic on its water.

A bargeman is throwing a line to tie up at the Knoxville dock. While commercial freight shipping became a major part of the Tennessee River system, railroads and trucking in East Tennessee continued to dominate the freight industries.

This was another popular TVA poster that was seen throughout Knoxville and East Tennessee emphasizing the importance of the hydroelectric dam system in the region.

The success of TVA in taming the Tennessee River attracted the attention of allied nations around the world, especially in Central and South America. This image shows a Mexican delegation and a TVA official discussing the project in Knoxville's headquarters.

Knoxville workers at Watts Bar Dam take time out to mug for the camera. The Watts Bar Dam was vital to the development of Oak Ridge and the massive amounts of energy the city would need for projects crucial to the nation's defense.

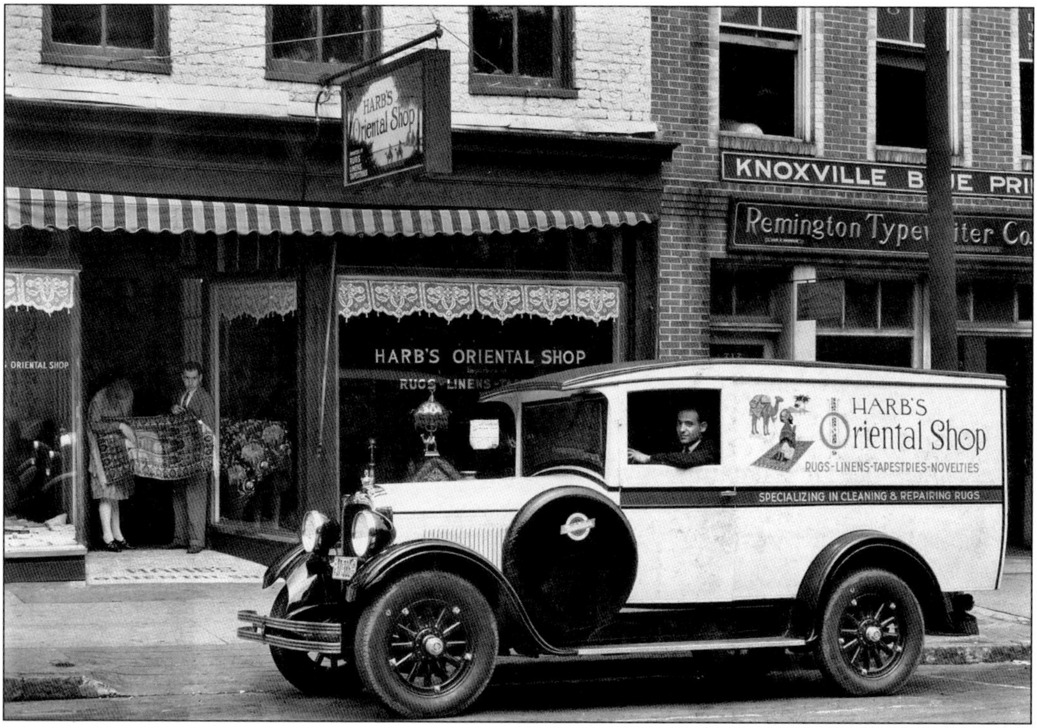

Harb's Oriental Shop was founded by John J. and W. J. Harb in Knoxville in 1926. The family immigrated to the city from Syria and became a fixture in the city's downtown business district. Workers moving to the Knoxville/Oak Ridge area during World War II made it one of the more popular places to shop downtown.

Pease Furniture in South Knoxville started as a grocery store in 1929 and began selling furniture full-time 10 years later. The business was a longtime fixture in the city and a supporter of many programs in the community of Vestal, especially its sponsorship of youth sporting teams.

This photograph was taken of the Pease family in the 1940s. From left to right are son Ardist Pease, father Joe Pease, mother Ama Pease, and son William Pease.

This is the Pease Furniture Company as it appeared in the 1940s. The ALCOA plant in nearby Maryville during World War II led to a growth in residents in South Knoxville's Vestal community. The family business was also a major supporter of youth athletic leagues in the city.

The Vestal Merchants (*c.* 1939) was a baseball team from the South Knoxville community. It was a popular pastime in the city. Neighborhoods and communities formed teams and played each other. This team was sponsored and supported by local businessmen in Vestal. The majority of those pictured here would see service in World War II.

The White Lily Flower Company was a major supplier of food to both the United States and the troops overseas. The company also produced its own coffee. During World War II, the plant almost doubled its output to meet the demands of the marketplace.

It wasn't just the big companies that served Knoxville in World War II. Agatha Smith founded the Burlington Flower Shop in 1939 and became a leader in the local floral business during the war years.

This photograph of the docks shows downtown Knoxville in the background. The support industries that sprang up because of the rise in river traffic had the potential to make commercial waterfront development a reality in Knoxville. It was hoped the river would become a major transportation avenue for companies in the region, and docks were built to accommodate the commercial barges carrying sand, stone, and other products on the inland waterways.

Two

Rallying to the Cause

Charitable organizations often find it difficult in good economic times to collect donations. In the cash-strapped years of World War II, it was as bad as it could get, but Knoxville residents did give. Those who couldn't spare money donated their efforts and helped the less fortunate when natural disasters and hard times struck.

The churches of Knoxville were staying busy helping their congregations when they could, but resources were severely limited beyond the offering plate and poor boxes. Others had to turn to organizations like the Red Cross and the Salvation Army for help. Government programs were scarce, underfunded, or too new to have direct impact on the population.

The Tennessee Valley Authority's community development programs extended beyond the jobs they offered to thousands of local residents. The organization was a major player in job training for unskilled workers and high-school students in the region. The training applied not only to their projects, but to the growing needs in the machining industry.

Rallying to the cause, however, meant more than aiding Tennessee's poor. There was a government to run, a city and county that required vigilance to make sure things operated smoothly during these trying times. This required the efforts of individuals as much as it did organizations. Some workers left their native city and moved to other parts of the nation where they did vital work in factories and shipyards. Others who volunteered for combat in the army ended up stateside assisting soldiers returning from overseas or teaching those going over.

The activation of the National Guard and the call up of men into the armed forces also left the region vulnerable to outside threats. With the Japanese attack on Pearl Harbor and the capture of German saboteurs on the East Coast, Knoxville and East Tennessee had to rely on the Tennessee State Guard for the defense and security of sensitive government projects that dotted the region.

The state guard had almost overnight become one of Tennessee's most relied upon security forces for protection of war-essential industries and as a support vehicle for local police. Tennessee put real effort into developing the guard, and their success was often found in the number of men recruited from their ranks into the regular military. In relation to the population, the state guard was the largest in the nation. They were the first to be federally trained and did their jobs without benefit of pay.

The Tennessee State Guard answered only to the governor. Their job in World War II was to stand in for the National Guard in their absence, secure the state from outside threats, and stand by to break up worker strikes in war-essential industries. Because of the TVA projects on the Tennessee River and the building of Oak Ridge, the guard maintained a highly visible presence in Knoxville.

The Knoxville Chapter of the American Red Cross maintained a strong stateside presence in World War II. Here members of the chapter are seen participating in a parade downtown in 1942. In addition to serving as messengers from wounded soldiers to their loved ones back home, Red Cross workers served in a variety of local functions, including volunteering as policemen to fill the ranks of Knoxville police called up for active duty.

In the 1940s, the Red Cross was called up to assist residents left homeless by flash flooding in rural areas of Knox County. This photograph shows a volunteer pulling a mother and her children to safety.

Local Boy Scouts assisted the Knoxville Red Cross in a fund-raising drive in the city. The organization included community service work in their Scouting program, which allowed them to earn badges of distinction for assisting charities.

Red Cross volunteers inspect food sent to them by local farmers in the L&N Train Yards. The produce is being loaded into a boxcar for distribution to those needing help. The organization stayed busy in World War II tending to the needs of families in crisis.

Central High School graduate and former University of Tennessee assistant football coach Wymer George "Petie" Siler served as a Red Cross assistant field director. He was a veteran of World War I and a popular coach in Morristown when he volunteered to go overseas in 1942 at age 47. He served with the 127th Infantry of the 32nd Division, seeing action in New Guinea, North Africa, and the Philippines. His work overseas in close combat with the troops earned him numerous commendations from the 127th Infantry. After the war, he resumed his decorated career as a coach in Morristown.

Knox County Public Schools also lent their hand to the war effort through the Stair Technical School in North Knoxville. It was a school where high-school-age children were sent to learn a trade. Former school board member Fred R. Stair, who served as mayor in 1942 and 1943, started it as away to offer students who weren't planning on a college career the opportunity to learn a trade.

As this photograph shows, students were trained on a variety of tools and equipment. The school was supported by local business owners and the Tennessee Valley Authority in terms of equipment donated and jobs provided to graduates. Some of Stair Tech's classes were held in downtown Knoxville.

Companies such as the Aluminum Company of America, TVA, Dempster Brothers, and Fulton Sylphon required the skilled labor the school provided. In addition, Stair Technical School was one of the first in the state to include women in its high-school industrial training programs. It would later be named Fulton High School in honor of Knoxville inventor Westin Fulton.

This is a photograph of Major and Mrs. James Shipp of the Knoxville Salvation Army. Major Shipp ran the Knoxville chapter in the late 1930s and early 1940s, which laid the groundwork for the chapter's success in World War II aiding the homeless and others in need.

While the Salvation Army attended to local needs, Salvation Army personnel from Knoxville were often assigned to assist with morale and USO tours in the Southeast and overseas. The programs were among the most popular with troops. In addition, the Salvation Army ministered to servicemen and acted as a voice to home in many cases. (Photograph courtesy of the Salvation Army Southern Historical Center.)

This is a group portrait of participants in a Kentucky-Tennessee-Arkansas Division Sectional Home League Rally at the Knoxville, Tennessee, corps in 1943. The large call up of soldiers in the three-state region meant larger challenges for the Home League, especially among poorer families in the region, where many breadwinners were drafted into military service. (Photograph courtesy of the Salvation Army Southern Historical Center.)

This is a group portrait of children under a tent at Vacation Bible School taken in 1943 in Knoxville. The photograph shows the children who attended and instructors—including corps officers Capt. and Mrs. D. Frank Hall at the rear.

Local churches aided and assisted with the war effort on numerous fronts. They held fundraisers for local families in need and helped sponsor drives for rubber, glass, and other needed wartime materials. This is a photograph of Immaculate Conception Church in Knoxville, whose congregation was known for its assistance in salvage drives.

Temple Beth-El saw considerable growth in World War II. It is Knoxville's oldest Jewish temple and was founded in the city in 1864. The Reformed Judaism congregation was a vibrant part of the city's economic, social, and political life. While numerous members of the Temple would serve in World War II in various branches of the armed forces, the building of Oak Ridge would attract many Jewish scientists and engineers to the region, who would join the congregation.

Another source of employment for Knoxvillians was the U.S. Navy shipyards in Charleston during World War II, where shifts operated around the clock. From left to right, the USS *James E. Craig* and the USS *Charles E. Eichenberger* are launched after being christened by the widows of the men for whom the ships are named.

Knoxville garage owner W. E. Hooper was called up by the U.S. Army to train African American convoy drivers at Fort Lee, Virginia, for Europe. During his service, he invented a device that allowed a single driver to change tandem tires. It increased the efficiency of convoy units. The unit he was training would go on to become known as the "Red Ball Express."

Hooper's oldest son, Dennis, volunteered for the U.S. Army when he was 15. He was found to have a talent for radio codes and was assigned to the Army Air Corps. He taught code stateside and worked in communications.

Frank Anderson left Knoxville for Amertorp Corporation outside of Chicago. The company was devoted entirely to manufacturing torpedoes. These are the airborne variety minus the warheads. The company was the largest industrial plant in the nation and drew other Knoxvillians to the factory.

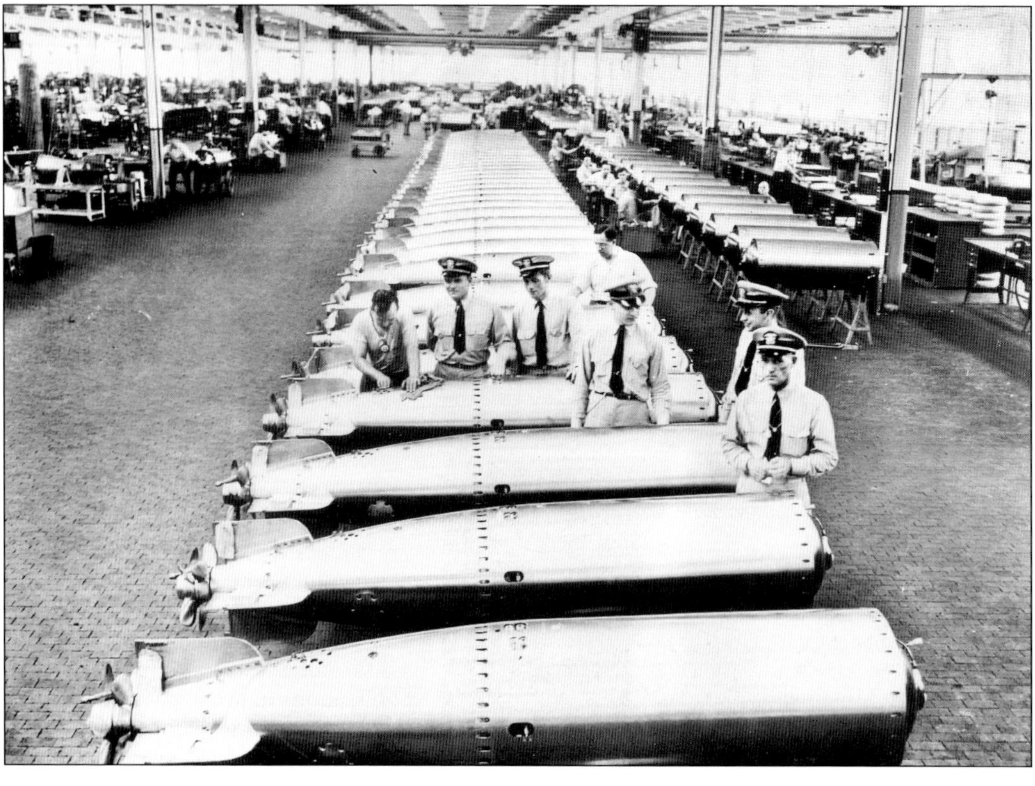

Knoxville native Johnny Harb Sr., son of Harb's Oriental Shop cofounder, served in the U.S. Army as a medic. He was assigned to stateside duty throughout the war, however, assisting soldiers returning from the battlefields.

Knoxvillian Boyd Browder was a prolific photographer of the city's black community. He was known for his photographs of African American life in the region and worked for a number of prominent publications in World War II. (Photograph courtesy of the Beck Cultural Exchange Center.)

Knoxville native William Henry Hasty served as an assistant to Secretary of War Henry Stimson during World War II. Hasty was the first African American federal judge in American history. At the onset of the draft, minorities were often assigned to noncombat positions, building runways and doing other construction jobs. Hasty fought military and federal officials to allow African Americans to be assigned to combat duty in World War II. (Photograph courtesy of the Beck Cultural Exchange Center.)

William Hasty (second from left) is seen here with Pres. Harry S. Truman. He was successful in his quest to get African Americans assigned to combat duty but resigned in protest when they were segregated from other soldiers. Hasty would go on to serve as the first black governor of Puerto Rico and see his quest realized when Truman desegregated the U.S. Armed Forces after World War II. (Photograph courtesy of the Beck Cultural Exchange Center.)

The Tennessee State Guard is seen here training their volunteers on how to disarm rioters. The state guard was expected to be able to deal with domestic riots and act as strike-breakers should employees walk out or try to strike against their employers in war-essential industries in World War II.

Because of the rural locations where the state guard was needed, they had to be trained like regular troops in the field. This is a bivouac operation where troops were learning how to establish a base camp. The guard was also trained on how to deal with poisonous gases, sabotage attempts at dams being built, and security at government installations in Oak Ridge.

Three

Heading Back to Europe

In a statement of service credits completed through November 11, 1944, and prepared for the Tennessee National Guard Adjutant General's office, the Selective Service Board reported that 21,765 Knox County residents were serving in the armed forces. By August 1945, that number would be more than 24,000 and climbing. The growth of TVA, the establishment of Oak Ridge, and ALCOA had brought in a considerable number of new residents to the county. The population, however, was still just a little more than 100,000 for Knox County. That made the 24,000 soldiers serving a staggering number to take into account.

The war in Europe attracted everyone's attention. For more than two years, most Knoxvillians had followed the war in Europe and the bombing of Great Britain. The coverage on radio and in the press told them of the rising German threat. When the bombs began falling in London, some Knoxvillians enlisted immediately for what they knew would eventually follow.

World War II in Europe was an entirely different conflict in nature than the First World War most had grown up hearing about from their fathers and grandfathers, but the real estate was the same. These soldiers, however, knew it would take more than their legendary skills with firearms to win it. They would be up against a military power in Germany that was battle-hardened from its conquests in Europe and more advanced in weaponry, tanks, planes, and—judging by their victories—tactics.

The Tennessee National Guard would once again be a major part of the 30th Division, which rose to military fame in World War I for their actions in the trenches. The division was reassigned numerous times. They would maintain their tradition of excellence, however, and become known in World War II as "Roosevelt's Shock Troops" for their actions under fire.

Unlike the war in the Pacific, the press coverage in Europe was more intense. National news networks and newspaper correspondents had been there for more than five years covering it. Families with loved ones overseas could turn on their radios every night to listen to the latest news or read about it the next day in the local papers. World War II was also the first time a war would be photographically documented by the common soldier. While families back home may not have been able to afford cameras or film, some soldiers from Knoxville did or knew someone who had one, which enabled them to bring home photographs from the front that recorded their service overseas.

Those that have survived the generations of time tell the small stories of the war in Europe that are often forgotten when the final text is written.

This photograph of Everett Parker and his cousin, Paul, was taken on Gay Street. Paul, who's face is obscured, is seen behind Everett. According to Everett, an unknown photographer would set his camera up on Knoxville's main thoroughfare every weekend and take photographs of people walking downtown. He would later sell those photographs as postcards.

This is another photograph of Everett (left) on Gay Street with longtime friend Sherman Cleveland. What makes the Parkers noteworthy to the city is that Everett had three other brothers at or near his age. Everett, Claude, Sam, and Fred were all drafted into the war. The first three were all part of the 7th Army. The fourth brother, Fred, served in the Pacific and was wounded in the Philippines.

PFC Claude Parker, pictured here, was in the D-Day Invasion and among the first waves of soldiers to land in France and begin the push towards Germany. He would see action in most of the campaigns on the continent.

Claude Parker (standing) poses with a friend identified as "William" in the photograph. Parker was an avid photographer while overseas and took a number of pictures of his fellow soldiers and the places they were stationed.

The Parker brothers were in France within days of each other. Claude Parker took this shot at the Eiffel Tower in Paris while visiting the city on liberty.

This is the 36th Division camp outside of Paris. The French chateau in the background served as a headquarters for a German unit prior to the Allied capture of the city.

Claude Parker is shown at base camp (fourth from left) with fellow soldiers following action near Paris, France. The reader can see the laundry hanging from the lines and the smokestacks on the tents. Although they were near some of the more modern cities in Europe, the soldiers' tents were their home overseas.

The same crew is ready to go out on liberty call and get some rest and recreation. The soldiers rarely got time to go out to see the cities in Europe, and it was a precious commodity they took seriously.

Claude Parker, who was in the invasion of Marseilles, France, took this photograph of an Allied ship in Marseilles Harbor. Because of the damage inflicted on European shipping by German U-boat activities, it was rare to see a big ship in the harbor. Most commercial vessels that survived during the war were at one time or another used for military service.

The Russian capture of Berlin forced many residents to flee the city, taking whatever they could carry. This photograph by Claude Parker shows a young woman pushing a baby carriage and a man behind her pulling a cart.

Everett Parker stands at the same fountain in Europe where his brother Claude was photographed three months earlier. The brothers met up quite often in Europe during the ensuing campaigns against Germany.

This is the third Parker brother, Sam, in uniform. During the war in Europe, the three brothers managed to escape serious injury or capture and returned home to Knoxville.

Knoxville native Torrence Popejoy served with the 614th Ordinance Company. He is seen here with Bill Hearn in the sidecar of a French motorcycle. Popejoy was in maintenance and supply and saw action in France and England during World War II.

This is a photograph of Torrence Popejoy taken next to a German Tiger tank in France in early 1945. The tanks were almost unbeatable on the battlefield in tank-to-tank matches with U.S. forces, and it was a considered a victory when one was destroyed in combat.

Knoxville native Charles B. LaRue served in North Africa and Italy. He was a tank commander during the war and saw some of the most brutal action as German and Italian forces tried to repel Allied invasions of the two continents.

LaRue participated in the invasion of Oran in North Africa. Here the American flag is raised at Oran and is flying over piles of war materiel being taken ashore from Allied ships to assist with the invasion.

U.S. soldiers in Africa made camp and pitched their pup tents on the outskirts of the cities. Tent cities like this one dotted North Africa throughout the campaign against the Axis armies. A soldier's backpack, including the half-shelter tent seen here, would weigh around 40 pounds or more depending on the amount of ammunition and equipment carried.

An Allied ship is anchored in the Port of Casablanca. The Battle of North Africa pitted American and British forces against Germany's Field Marshall Erwin Rommel—regarded as one of the best tactical minds of the German army.

One of the best ways to lift troop morale was baseball. This baseball game was played with soldiers from the field. Here the pitcher throws from the plate.

The batter bunts the ball down and is already leaning toward first base. Games such as this were the best stress relievers for the players, who got a chance to relive their youth and have a good time.

Charles LaRue stands next to his tank in Italy. After the battles in North Africa, LaRue would serve out the war in Italy and be stationed near Rome. After the war, he would join the Salvation Army and rise through the ranks to become a major. He served in a variety of posts before retiring to his native Knoxville.

C. B. LaRue was 12 miles away on base when Mount Vesuvius erupted on March 1944. The volcano observatory was being used as a command post for the region. The lava destroyed the U.S. planes stationed at Terzigno, several villages, and 88 B-25 bombers.

Here Allied forces march a squad of captured German POWs to an internment camp in Italy following a battle where LaRue participated.

American soldiers and pilots look over a downed German plane to recover any parts or pieces of it that can be used. Aircraft parts were in short supply in the Italian theater of operations, and every downed plane was combed from front to back looking for things that would work on Allied aircraft.

This is the 17th General Hospital in Italy. Soldiers serving with LaRue had to watch for German booby traps when the Allied forces first took control of it. Wounded German soldiers were discovered in a tunnel used to transport the wounded to hospital beds. .

The soldiers graveyard located on the 17th General Hospital grounds. Soldiers from Italy and Germany were buried here during the war.

A common sight for many Knoxvillians stationed in Italy was Pope Pius XII. He had assumed the papacy in 1939 and would often visit the 17th General Hospital, where he would bless the wounded soldiers and shake hands with them.

While Pope Pius XII was often criticized for maintaining neutrality at the Vatican during World War II, it was later discovered that by doing so the Vatican could serve as a refuge for war victims.

Knoxville native Lt. Edward Cothren was serving on the front lines in Italy when he was killed in combat. He was serving in a U.S. Army unit known as the Buffalo Soldiers, named after the highly decorated all-black cavalry units in the American West. Lieutenant Cothren's death on the battlefields of Italy entered him in the history books of Knoxville as the first African American Knoxvillian to be killed in World War II. (Photograph courtesy of the Beck Cultural Exchange Center.)

U.S. Army soldiers inspect a bullet-riddled German JU88 warplane that was shot down in the Battle of Sicily. Second from the left is noted Knoxville native Lt. Fred G. Ramsey. His family operated the Ramsey Cafeteria downtown, which remains a Knoxville landmark.

This previously unpublished photograph of Gen. George Patton in field gear and with a fresh cigar was shot as he went over the side of the boat that carried him from North Africa to the shores of Sicily.

General Patton (seen in the middle) wades knee-deep into the surf as he goes ashore in Sicily to rally his force for the attack against Axis forces. The film being shot by the cameraman to the left would be the official government film released telling American audiences back home about the invasion of the Italian island.

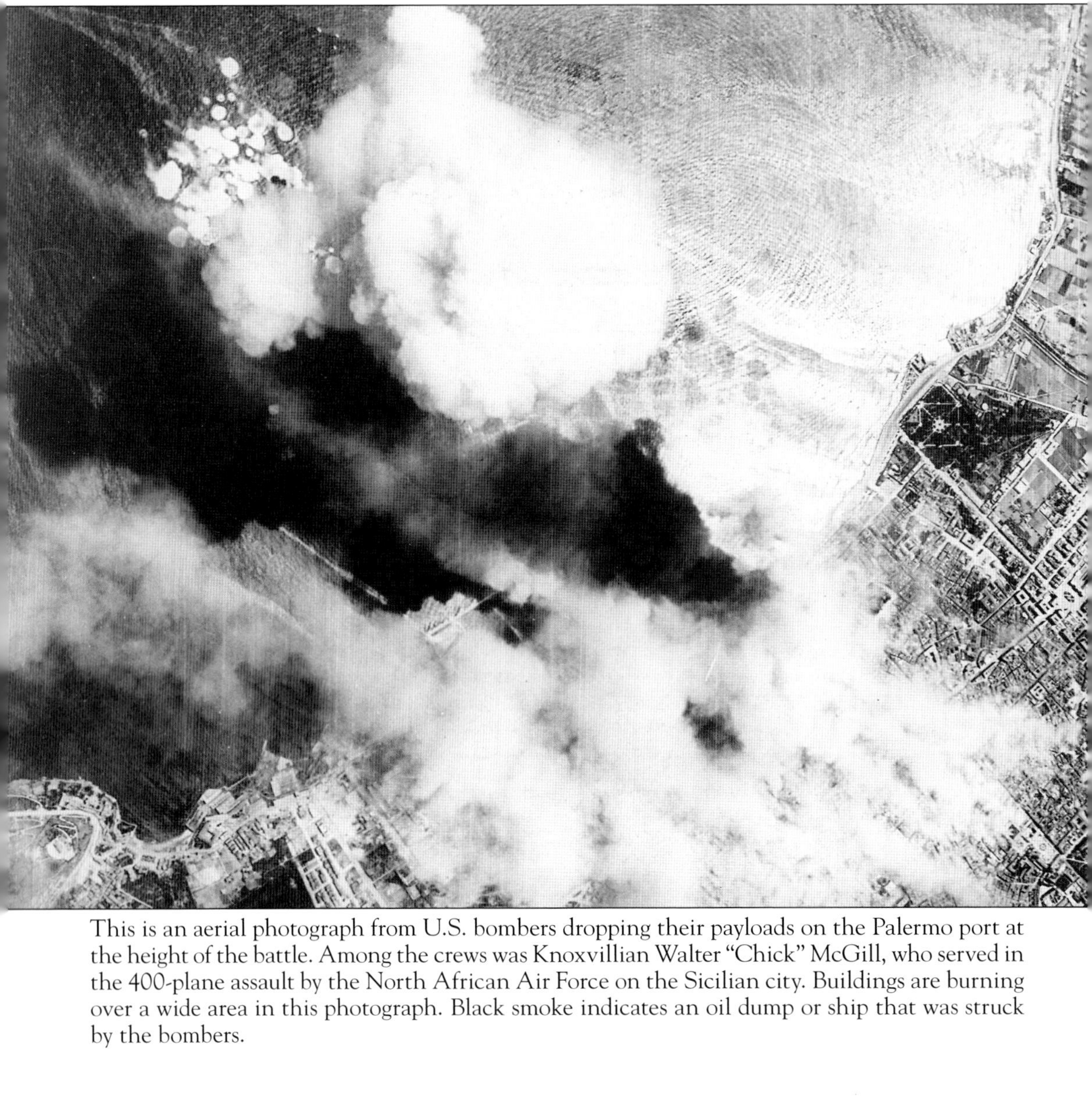

This is an aerial photograph from U.S. bombers dropping their payloads on the Palermo port at the height of the battle. Among the crews was Knoxvillian Walter "Chick" McGill, who served in the 400-plane assault by the North African Air Force on the Sicilian city. Buildings are burning over a wide area in this photograph. Black smoke indicates an oil dump or ship that was struck by the bombers.

Soldiers drive past citizens after the fall of Palermo, Sicily, to American forces in 1943. The citizens filled the streets of the city after the Americans passed through. In this photograph, they are waving an American flag in support of the troops that passed by them.

This photograph shows four Knoxville African Americans in the Italian campaigns holding a briefing. From left to right are Master Sgt. Jack Alexander, Lieutenant Sims, Lieutenant Porter, and First Lieutenant Ross. Very few photographs of the black soldiers from Knoxville exist, and only a handful of pictures survive in the hands of family members.

South Knoxville resident and U.S. Army Air Corps tech Sgt. Walter "Chick" McGill prepares for a mission. His 390th Heavy Bombardment Group shot down more planes and flew more missions than any other in Europe. He received the Distinguished Flying Cross and three Bronze Stars, while his group received a Presidential Citation for their service in the war.

With a Flying Fortress in the background, members of the U.S. Army's 8th Air Force take time out to plant a garden at the edge of a runway in northern England. The base mess hall was one of its best features, as the pilots planted a 40-acre garden that produced vegetables in season for the mess hall menu.

Eighth Army Air Corps general Nathan B. Forrest III was flying a bombing mission over Germany when his B-17 was shot down. His crew made it to the North Sea before being forced to ditch the plane. Only one of the crewmen survived. It wasn't until after World War II that the body of Confederate general Nathan B. Forrest's great-grandson was returned to Arlington National Cemetery for burial.

This image of Morristown native Jack Goan was taken in 1944. He served as a belly gunner on a B-17 bomber in Europe. He is credited with downing several planes, including a German jet. He is regarded as one of the first men to have shot down a jet fighter.

This is the landing zone at Normandy following the invasion. The sea transports brought in troops and equipment for days during the Allied forces' establishment of a beachhead.

Two soldiers stand next to a jeep while troops and equipment are being off-loaded on shore. In the background, you can see the armband of a medic helping transport a soldier wounded in the invasion to a hospital ship.

This photograph was found in the Jerry Mayes collection and is labeled "unidentified Knoxvillian Germany 1945." The soldier is standing next to a half-track with a pistol on his side. It was common in the war when soldiers saw another American with a camera to ask for a photograph to be taken to send home.

Knoxville attorney Earl Ailor volunteered for service in the U.S. Army in World War II. He attained the rank of captain while serving with the 9th Infantry Division. He saw service in the Normandy invasion and the Battle of the Bulge. Ailor would also later serve as a member of the Judge Advocates Office in Europe.

This group of unidentified officers is standing outside a building in France. Ailor is believed to be fifth from the left. The 9th Division was in the thick of the fighting in Europe and fought their way through France to Berlin.

South Knoxville native Walter A. Chambers entered the U.S. Army in 1942 and served with a tank destroyer unit in Europe. He saw action at the Battle of the Bulge and received a Purple Heart for injuries sustained in the battle.

Knoxvillian Philip Moss is seen here on the right. He volunteered with the army in World War II just after the attack on Pearl Harbor. During basic training, he was close enough to his mother's home to leave training to eat dinner.

Moss took this photograph of a soldier leaning against his fighting vehicle during a break in the Battle of the Bulge. Moss volunteered into the service following the attack on Pear Harbor and was in Europe from the Normandy Invasion to the fall of Berlin.

Moss was assigned to the 6th Division. Here his tank crew takes a moment to check on equipment and do some routine maintenance en route to Berlin. The Americans were driving into the western side while the Russians were coming in from the east.

This is Moss standing next to his half-track in Germany. The University of Tennessee graduate often acted as a scout for the division and was among the first to bring back news to his commanders about finding the concentration camp near Nuremberg that the 6th Army liberated.

Soldiers find cover in the shadow of a bombed-out building during the Rheinland campaign to smoke a cigarette.

The 6th Division built this pontoon bridge over the Rhein River in Germany. Engineers with the 6th Division were among some of the best in the field and could put a bridge over a body of water in hours. The convoy rolling over it shows the sturdiness the structure.

Although American troops halted 60 miles west of Berlin while the Russian army captured the city, the full force of the Allied army paraded through it in the victory celebration that followed. These are Moss's 6th Division tanks rolling in column during the parade. He would be stationed in the city for months after the fall of Berlin.

An unidentified British regiment marches in the same parade through the city of Berlin. The July 1945 parade was attended by officials and heads of state throughout Europe.

This photograph was taken by Moss at the Berlin parade of the commanding generals standing in review of their respective troops. At far left is American commander Gen. George S. Patton.

The "maintenance gang" is photographed in Berlin following the capture of the city. After so long on campaign, the 6th Division maintenance crews worked overtime to get their vehicles back in shape and ready to move.

Although the campaign across Germany was brutal, Moss found some comfort at the end of the trail in his new quarters. This hotel is where he and his men made their home while stationed in Germany.

Knoxvillian Dennis Hooper took this photograph of Pres. Franklin D. Roosevelt and European commanding general Dwight Eisenhower in the back of the jeep at a stateside event in World War II.

Full-blooded Cherokee Goingback Chitoskie was a master carver and model maker who joined the Army Corps of Engineers in 1942. He worked on a number of classified projects, including making the terrain maps for the Battle of North Africa, the Normandy Invasion, and bombing targets in the Pacific. In addition, he carved the working model of what would become the landing ship tank (LST).

Four

The Asian Campaigns

As World War II progressed into 1942 and 1943, it seemed more and more Knoxvillians were being sent to serve in the war in the Pacific. Unlike Europe, the old continent that every American schoolchild had grown up learning about, Asia and Japan were a different story. The island geography was simply places on a map for most people in Knoxville, and very few understood how entrenched the Japanese had become in the region over the last generation.

For almost a year after the attack on Pearl Harbor, U.S. forces were in a defensive position fighting to keep what little real estate Allied forces had prior to the attack. The Battle of Midway finally turned the war in America's favor, but now came the brutal task of an island-by-island campaign to push the Japanese back to their homeland and defeat them. It was a task that fell on commanding general Douglas MacArthur, a man of legend to many East Tennesseans. His roots in the state went back to the Civil War. His father had earned the Medal of Honor during the Battle of Chattanooga, and General MacArthur's wife, Jean, was a Rutherford County, Tennessee, native who was known to many in the state.

Families in Knoxville with loved ones in the Pacific recall reading newspapers and listening to radio broadcasts with a globe or world map in their hands to see where their sons were fighting with MacArthur. Some of the islands and tolls where the action was fiercest sometimes could not be found on the simple maps they possessed. The soldiers from Knoxville who fought in the Pacific remember the European war dominating the nation's resources and headlines back home. Even among correspondents, there was a learning curve that sometimes made reporting what news they could of the war effort a difficult task, which made it harder for the families back home in East Tennessee trying to keep track of their loved ones.

The Pacific theater, however, would be the one where Knoxvillians would earn their greatest victories and honors. It would also be the one that resulted in a majority of the city's casualties and deaths in World War II.

Knoxvillian Fred Parker is seen here on the right. He served in the 42nd Rainbow Division and fought in the battles to retake the Philippines. He was the only Parker brother to see action in the Pacific. In the battle for Luzon, he would be critically injured by chemicals and carry the scars of it for the rest of his life.

Because of the devastating effect on the Pacific fleet in the attack on Pear Harbor, the U.S. Navy relied on a guerilla naval craft known as a PT boat. The torpedo boats were so successful and easy to build that the navy built them alongside the regular ships. This is Archbishop Joseph Rummel at the New Orleans shipyard standing on the deck of a newly constructed torpedo boat and blessing it during a commissioning ceremony.

Many Knoxvillians worked at the Newport News, Virginia, shipyard. Here workmen who helped build the new USS *Hornet* take a last look at the aircraft carrier before it is launched in 1943. The original *Hornet*, which carried Gen. Jimmy Doolittle and his crew in their bombing mission over Tokyo, was sunk in the Santa Cruz Islands a year earlier. The speed at which the workmen built the new flattop was amazing.

Secretary of the Navy Frank Cox leans against the bow of the USS *Hornet* as his wife, Annie Reid, christens it with a bottle of champagne. Because of the fame of the *Hornet*, news of the launching was carried across the nation.

Charlie Burchett volunteered into the U.S. Marine Corps at the onset of the war. Because of his engineering training, Burchett was placed in the USMC combat engineers. He served in numerous battles overseas, including Peleliu and Guadalcanal. Here he is seen at Pavuvu in the Russell Islands playing a game of pick-up baseball.

Burchett is seen here second from the left with a native guide. Marine combat engineers were among the best soldiers to have in the field. They established field bases, served as infantry, and checked for mines and explosives.

A large group of sailors gather at Duffy's Tavern at a navy recreation center on an island near the Solomons. Former Notre Dame football standout and "Four Horseman" Lt. Cmdr. Jim Crowley supervised the recreation center. The center was one of the only places for sailors and marines to

have liberty. The island where the center was located also served as a staging area for planning invasions on the neighboring islands.

Charlie Burchett with knife in hand is stirring the fire as he prepares his evening meal on Peleliu. The .45 sidearm he carried in his shoulder holster was used for "cave clearing" operations, where he and a partner would go into the darkened caves to check for enemy troops.

Burchett is standing in full jungle gear as he poses for this photograph on Peleliu. The Knoxvillian would return to the city, where he would become the dean of student conduct at the University of Tennessee and an ardent supporter of veterans' programs.

South Knoxville resident and U.S. Army Sgt. Troy McGill volunteered for service in World War II and became the city's only native Medal of Honor recipient. Gen. Douglas MacArthur personally awarded the medal to his family at Fort Sill, Oklahoma. At the Battle of Los Negros Island, he is credited with single-handedly defending an airstrip and killing more than 100 Japanese soldiers. Army investigators would later report that the majority had been killed in hand-to-hand combat.

This is a view of the Battle of Wake Island under attack by American forces. From a plane at low altitude can be seen two damaged surface ships; the black smoke is shielding the Japanese planes that were destroyed on the ground.

Flight deck crews swarm over the bombers returning from Wake Island in the 1943 attack. The planes had just returned from a bombing run on the island. Readers can see in the foreground where an enemy bullet has hit the plane's right wing.

Six two-engined Japanese bombers burn near the runways on Peacock Point. The coordinated attack by American planes and ships claimed 31 enemy planes, and 30 more were shot down out of the sky in aerial combat.

These navy pilots have just returned from the Wake Island battle. They swapped stories and grabbed something to eat before seeing to their planes.

A fire started during the navy's bombardment of Wake Island burns out of control near the island's airfield. In the foreground of the photograph are the remains of a Japanese ship that was beached a year earlier when the Japanese captured the island.

Maj. Ernest Harris of nearby Morristown, Tennessee, flew a P-40 Warhawk in the Southwest Pacific theater. Gen. Douglas MacArthur commended his 49th Fighter Group as being "unsurpassed in the air." The ace pilot was credited with 11 kills and 8 probable kills in the dogfights over New Guinea.

Another popular plane with flat-tops was the Grumman "Wildcat." They are greeted here by flight crews and pushed back into position. The folding wing gave carriers the space to add more planes to their stock.

While planes and ships were stock in trade for the navy, the success of the PT boat fleets in sinking enemy ships led the navy to research and study a way to build faster and more powerful small boats. This experimental craft was part of the navy's research and is resting on Dempster pontoons built in Knoxville.

Knoxvillian Edward Kirkland, seen kneeling far right, joined the U.S. Marine Corps in World War II. He is operating a phonographic recorder while he gets his comrades from Michigan and Minnesota to sing; he then mailed copies of the record they made back home to their families.

S2c. R. H. Holloway of Knoxville, seen far right, and his fellow sailors are cleaning and oiling a gun mount in port.

William Pease of Pease Furniture in South Knoxville joined the U.S. Army in 1942. After training, he saw action in New Guinea. The Battle of New Guinea is largely forgotten by historians but is regarded as one of the most vicious battles in the Pacific. It is the second largest island in the world and was firmly held by the Japanese.

Here soldiers march through a pass in New Guinea. Malaria and other tropical diseases were the biggest enemies to Allied forces. American, Australian, and British forces combined in a two-year effort to seize the island. Some 24,000 casualties were reported among Allied forces in the campaign.

In a solemn ceremony, U.S. Marines honor their dead at Viru Harbor in the New Georgia islands. A 21-gun salute is fired to honor the fallen Marines. The 4th Marine Raider Battalion led the attack on the island, which was central to the Solomon and New Guinea campaigns. There were

close to 20,000 Japanese troops on New Georgia and nearby Kolombangara Island. After a hard 10-day battle, the Marines captured Viru Harbor with little resistance. The Marines were still in camouflage dress when they took time to pay homage to their fallen comrades.

Soldiers resupply before marching out in New Guinea. The high heat and humidity of the jungle took its toll on soldiers.

Knoxvillian Tommy Walker entered the U.S. Navy and served on the USS *Yorktown*. The crew was required to do daily calisthenics as part of their service aboard ship. It was a daily routine for the ship's crew right up to the day of attack.

Jeff Claborne of Morristown served in the U.S. Army during World War II, serving in the Pacific theater until the Japanese surrender. He returned to Morristown after the war where he raised a family.

81
EXTINGUIS

Lt. Tom Dempster joined the U.S. Navy a year prior to the Japanese attack on Pearl Harbor and served as a navy pilot flying reconnaissance patrols. He is second from the left standing in Guadalcanal. This photograph was taken in 1943 prior to a visit by First Lady Eleanor Roosevelt. The black paint seen next to the plane's mascot had to be used to cover the plane's motto before she arrived. (Photograph courtesy of Tom Dempster.)

Knoxville attorney U.S. Army lieutenant James Ailor served with the 77th Infantry Division in the Pacific theater. He was part of the unit assaulting Le Shima in the Battle of Okinawa with famed journalist Ernie Pyle at his side. They came under fire and took cover in a nearby ditch when a sniper bullet killed the reporter. Lieutenant Ailor was also killed in the fighting three days later.

William W. McGill, brother of Walter "Chick" McGill, was gunnery captain on the oil tanker USS *Kanawha* when Japanese dive bombers attacked near Tulag Harbor. The ship was destroyed, and McGill was forced to abandon ship. Lieutenant and future-president John F. Kennedy witnessed the attack. The PT boats near the harbor retrieved McGill two hours later from the water.

McGill, right, was posted to the USS *Colorado* as its gunnery captain and, over the next three years, maintained his post as the ship engaged in some of the heaviest action of the war in the Pacific.

William McGill is fourth from the left in the back row of this family photograph taken in South Knoxville while on leave before he was shipped out to the *Colorado* again in 1944.

On July 24, 1944, the USS *Colorado* began shelling Tinian as a preinvasion tactic for troop support. The Japanese unleashed their shore batteries on the ship, hitting it 22 times, but the ship continued to fire. Allied ships watched in horror as the ship took the abuse and kept firing. Wes McGill took this photograph showing the damage to the 8-inch gun on Turret II.

This shows the damage done to the ship's 5.25-caliber gun after a direct hit by a Japanese 8-inch shell. During the attack, the exposed men on the ship's deck suffered serious casualties.

Wes McGill, seventh from left in the third row, is pictured here with the ship's 5th Division. The others identified in the photograph also in the third row are Lieutenant Popiel (eighth from left) and Lieutenant (JG) Beckham (ninth from left).

This is the gun crew on the USS *Colorado* taking time out from drilling and posing for a snapshot. The crews drilled every day to stay in shape at their battle stations.

McGill worked each crew on the guns under his direction. This shot was taken while undergoing repairs on the guns damaged by a kamikaze pilot during the battle at Leyte Gulf.

This is the gun crew in dress uniforms posing for a shot before taking liberty following the Battle of Okinawa.

The USS *Colorado* stayed in continuous combat operation throughout 1944 and 1945, logging more than 80,000 miles. This is a view astern of the *Colorado* as she steams toward Tokyo Bay for the Japanese surrender.

This is the water of Tokyo Bay, where the USS *Colorado* was invited to accompany the USS *Missouri*. During her time in World War II, the *Colorado* shot down more enemy planes than any other ship afloat and was given the honor of escorting the "Big Mo" to take the Japanese surrender.

After four years of brutal fighting, being blown from the USS *Kanawha*, and almost getting killed by a kamikaze pilot, McGill and sailors stand at attention in Yokohama, Japan, which is across the bay from Tokyo, get their first liberty call. McGill is eighth from the left in the first row.

The sight of Tokyo and Yokohama in ruins was a shock to most sailors disembarking to the city. The firebombing of the cities earlier in the year by the Army Air Corps had killed more people than the atomic bombs in Hiroshima and Nagasaki.

These are the ruins of the industrial section of Yokohama. Allied bombers aimed to hit the wartime production arm of Japan by dropping bombs on known factories in the city.

A transport truck carrying troops touring the city is in the foreground of this photograph taken by Wes McGill. This building in Tokyo shows the effects the firebombing had on even the most well-constructed buildings. The reader can see the blackened scarring on the outside walls.

This building was gutted by the Allied firebombing of Japan—making appearances deceiving to those looking at it. The outside wall of this apartment complex showed no damage, but the wood interior was destroyed.

An American jeep tries to navigate its way through Tokyo traffic. The city was remarkably ordered during the surrender ceremonies, and life seemed to go on as the nation recovered after the sudden peace.

An armored car patrols the streets of Tokyo. While the Allied forces had held back from Berlin so the Russian army could capture it, the Russians returned the favor with the Americans taking the surrender of Japan.

Sailors from the USS *Colorado* mingle outside a Japanese restaurant. The businesses in the city welcomed the American trade that came with the surrender after years of war.

This photograph was taken by Wes McGill of his gun crew standing at a road sign marking the ways to Tokyo and Yokohama. The *Colorado* remained in Tokyo in August and September, covering the surrender of the nation and giving the sailors a much-needed rest.

Her majesty's sailors and officer take a tour of the city of Tokyo. Within a month of the announcement of the surrender, tens of thousands of troops were in Japan. More than 100 ships, including Australian and British battleships, American submarines, and infantry craft, were present at the ceremonies.

A Japanese policeman on patrol in Yokohama watches the streets. Almost immediately after arriving in Tokyo Bay, the Americans made working arrangements with the local police to get them back on the streets performing their jobs. Before sailors disembarked from any ship in the bay during the surrender, they were ordered to observe the laws and customs of the Japanese people.

Two sailors from the *Missouri* take a rickshaw ride in Yokohama. For the majority of American sailors, the time spent in Japan during the surrender was the first exposure they had to Japanese culture.

Sailors from the *Missouri* and the *Colorado* mingle with each other after landing onshore. After her service in Tokyo Bay, the *Colorado* departed for the United States. The ship was decommissioned two years later and would spend the next 12 years in "mothballs" before being sold for scrap metal.

Former Knoxvillian Clifton B. Cates entered service during World War I while a student at the University of Tennessee. He rose to the rank of colonel in World War II, led the 1st Marine Regiment at Guadalcanal, and took command of the 4th Marine Division in the Marianas operation, the Tinian campaign, and the seizure of Iwo Jima. He would go on to become a general in the Marines and serve as its postwar commandant, where he led the fight to keep the Corps a separate fighting force.

This photograph of Gen. Douglas MacArthur and former Knoxvillian U.S. Army colonel Ross Hooper was taken following the surrender of Japan. MacArthur oversaw the surrender and rebuilding of the nation.

With the fighting ended in Europe and Asia, the next thing East Tennesseans wanted to see was this sight—dawn breaking over the Smoky Mountains. Marines, sailors, and soldiers returned home to waiting families, jobs, and an educational opportunity with the GI Bill that completely reshaped the city of Knoxville and East Tennessee forever.

BIBLIOGRAPHY

Amis, Reese T. *Knox County in the World War.* Knoxville: Knoxville Lithographic Company, 1919.

Deadrick, Lucille. *Heart of the Valley: A History of Knoxville, Tennessee.* Knoxville: East Tennessee Historical Society, 1976.

Rothrock, Mary. *The French Broad–Holston Country.* Knoxville: East Tennessee Historical Society, 1946.

Hooper, William E. *Tennessee History Classroom.* Knoxville: Tennessee Online, 1996.

———. *The Volunteer Chronicles.* Knoxville: Tennessee Online, 2001.

DISCOVER THOUSANDS OF LOCAL HISTORY BOOKS FEATURING MILLIONS OF VINTAGE IMAGES

Arcadia Publishing, the leading local history publisher in the United States, is committed to making history accessible and meaningful through publishing books that celebrate and preserve the heritage of America's people and places.

Find more books like this at
www.arcadiapublishing.com

Search for your hometown history, your old stomping grounds, and even your favorite sports team.

Consistent with our mission to preserve history on a local level, this book was printed in South Carolina on American-made paper and manufactured entirely in the United States. Products carrying the accredited Forest Stewardship Council (FSC) label are printed on 100 percent FSC-certified paper.

MADE IN THE USA